At Home with Science

Color and Noise!

Let's play with toys

Written by Janice Lobb
Illustrated by Peter Utton and Ann Savage

KINGFISHER
NEW YORK

KINGFISHER
Larousse Kingfisher Chambers Inc.
80 Maiden Lane
New York, New York 10038
www.kingfisherpub.com

First published in 2001
10 9 8 7 6 5 4 3 2 1

1TR/0501/FR/SC/128JDA

Created and designed by Snapdragon Publishing Ltd.
Copyright © Snapdragon Publishing Ltd. 2001

LIBRARY OF CONGRESS CATALOGING-IN-PUBLICATION DATA
has been applied for.

ISBN 0-7534-5362-2

Printed in Hong Kong

For Snapdragon
Editorial Director Jackie Fortey
Art Director Chris Legee
Designers Chris Legee and Joy Fitzsimons

For Kingfisher
Editors Jennie Morris and Emma Wild
Series Art Editor Mike Davis
DTP Manager Nicky Studdart
Production Controller Debbie Otter

Contents

About this book

Y̶ou may think that making music, painting your own masterpiece, or riding a bike has nothing to do with science—but it does! This book shows you how to make exciting discoveries while you are playing with your toys.

What if?

Where?

Which?

Why?

How?

Hall of Fame

Archie and his friends are here to help you. They are each named after a famous scientist—apart from Bob the (rubber) duck, who is a young scientist like you!

Archie
ARCHIMEDES (287–212 B.C.) The Greek scientist Archimedes figured out why things float or sink while he was in the bathtub. According to the story, he was so pleased that he leaped up, shouting "Eureka!" which means "I've done it!"

Frank
BENJAMIN FRANKLIN (1706–1790) Besides being one of the most important figures in American history, he was also a noted scientist. In a dangerous experiment in which he flew a kite in a storm, he proved that lightning is actually electricity.

Marie
MARIE CURIE (1867–1934) Girls did not go to college in Poland, where Marie Curie grew up, so she went to Paris to study. Later, she worked on radioactivity and received two Nobel prizes for her discoveries, in 1903 and 1911.

Dot
DOROTHY HODGKIN (1910–1994) Dorothy Hodgkin was a British scientist who made many important discoveries about molecules and atoms, the tiny particles that make up everything around us. She was given the Nobel prize for Chemistry in 1964.

See for yourself!

1 Read about the science in your playroom, then try the "See for yourself!" experiments to discover how it works. In science, experiments try to find or show the answers.

2 Carefully read the instructions for each experiment, making sure you follow the numbered steps in the correct order.

3 Here are some of the things you will need. Have everything ready before you start each experiment.

Mirrors

Cereal box

Salt

Matchboxes

Magnet

Building blocks

Bowl

Flour

Plastic tub

Penny

Thread spools

Yarn

Cardboard

Paper clip

Beads

Scissors

Tape

Buttons

Shoelaces

Colored pencils

4 ## Safety first! ✋

Some scientists took risks to make their discoveries, but our experiments are safe. Just make sure that you tell an adult what you are doing, and ask them for help when you see the red warning sign.

Amazing facts **WOW!**

You'll notice that some words are written in *italics*. You can learn more about them in the glossary at the end of the book. And if you want to find out some amazing facts, keep an eye out for the "Wow!" panels.

Keep an eye out for useful tips!

Have fun!

What are toys made of?

Children have played with toys for thousands of years. In the past, people made toys from any materials they could find. They were sewn from stuffed rags, *molded* from clay, carved from bone or wood, braided from straw, or made of metals like tin or lead. Some of these materials were not always safe for children to play with. Today, stores are full of toys that are bright, colorful, and safe to use. Many are still made from cloth, metal, and wood, but most toys are *mass-produced* using cheap, modern materials, such as *plastic*.

What happened to the wooden car?

It wooden go!

Toy factory

In a factory, large numbers of toys can be made at once. When plastic is heated, it becomes soft and can be molded into any shape or size. When plastic cools, it hardens and keeps the shape of the mold.

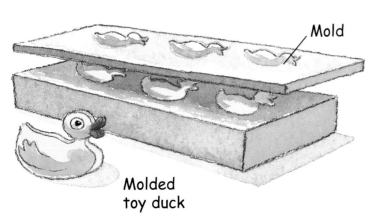

Mold

Molded toy duck

Mold

Red-hot metal is poured into a hole in the mold.

Like plastic, metal also becomes liquid when it is very hot and can be poured into molds to make toys. When it has cooled down, it can be painted.

6

See for yourself!

1 Which of your toys are soft? Figure out which ones are made of materials like rubber or cloth.

Rag doll

Rubber ball

Cloth teddy bear

2 Now figure out which are your metal toys. Metal is easy to spot because it is usually hard, cold, and shiny.

Car

Truck

Plane

3 Are any of your toys made of natural materials? Wood, cardboard, rope, and cotton cloth all come from trees and plants.

Cardboard jigsaw puzzle

Wood

Jump rope

Felt puppet

Rope

4 Most of your toys are probably made from man-made materials, like plastic. How many different shapes and colors can you find? Are the plastic toys hard or soft?

Blocks

Inflatable toy

Electronic toy

Yo-yo

WOW!

Boneshakers!

Bicycles weren't always as comfortable as they are today. This model from 1870 had wooden wheels. It was called a boneshaker because it gave people a very bumpy ride!

Look for the safety symbol!

What's in my box of paints?

What bow can't be untied?

A rainbow!

Each paint in your box of paints gets its color from a substance called a *pigment*. In daylight, we are able to see a pigment's true color. The sun's white light is a mixture of colored lights, which we can see when they are separated out in a rainbow. When sunlight falls on a pigment, some of the light is taken in, or *absorbed*. The color we see depends on what light is bounced off, or *reflected*, back to our eyes. For example, we say a pigment is green if it reflects green light and absorbs all other colors.

Seeing colors

Red, yellow, and blue are the three *primary colors*. You can make other colors by mixing them together.

A pigment that absorbs all the light falling on it, and does not reflect any back, looks black.

Blue and yellow make green.

Mixing all three colors together makes muddy black.

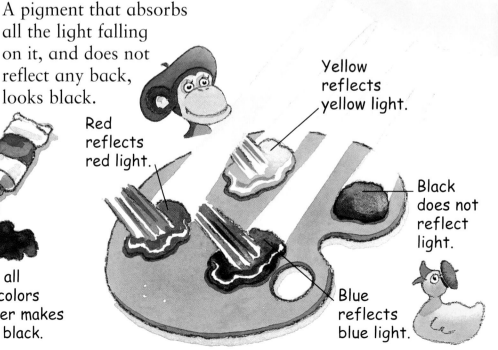

Red reflects red light.

Yellow reflects yellow light.

Black does not reflect light.

Blue reflects blue light.

8

See for yourself!

1 Divide a circle of white cardboard into three segments with a pencil, and color them red, yellow, and blue—the primary colors.

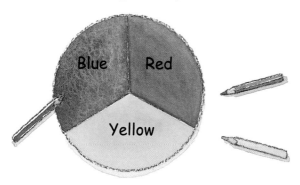

Blue Red

Yellow

2 Thread yarn or string through two small holes in the center of the circle. Use a large button to protect the holes.

Yarn

Button

3 Swing the disk around to twist the yarn, then pull the ends tight to make it spin. The colors go around so fast that your eyes can't keep up, so the cardboard looks gray!

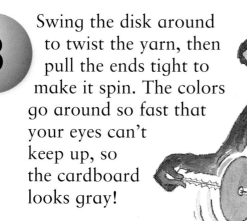

WOW! Prehistoric paint!

Today most of the pigments we use are man-made chemicals, but some natural colors have been used for thousands of years. Prehistoric people drew pictures of animals on cave walls with burned sticks and chalk, then painted them with colored soil and ground-up rocks.

Remember to clean your paintbrushes!

9

How do things stay up?

What did one wall say to the other?

Meet you at the corner!

You wouldn't expect people to use soft materials to make buildings. Buildings have to be made from materials that are not easily stretched, pulled, or squashed out of shape. They also have to be strong, so they do not break easily. Wood building blocks are stiff and strong. If you stand them on the floor, any *force* you put on them goes through them to the floor without making them change shape. But blocks made from foam rubber are not as stiff, and they squash when you push them.

Forces

Even a tall stack of blocks stays firm if the force pushing down on it is *vertical*. The tower doesn't fall over, and the blocks don't move because the floor pushes back.

Vertical force

Floor pushes back

One wall supports the other.

If the force on a stack of bricks is not vertical, it will fall sideways. Bricks stay up better if they are attached to another wall and if they are joined together.

The stiff walls and base of this dollhouse help each other stay standing up.

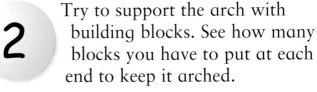

See for yourself!

1 Gently bend a piece of cardboard to form an arch. Will it stand up? The ends try to spread out and flatten the cardboard.

2 Try to support the arch with building blocks. See how many blocks you have to put at each end to keep it arched.

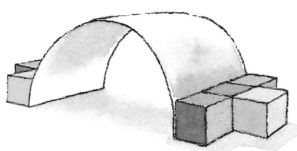

3 Rest some cardboard across the top of the arch, and support its ends. Stand a tin can in the middle.

The can's weight pushes the sides of the arch, not the middle.

4 Try to build the bridge again without the arch. The weight of the can will make the bridge collapse in the middle.

Thinking big!

WOW!

Tiny plastic bricks can be put together to make very large structures. Some theme parks contain model villages, towns, and whole landscapes made from thousands of toy bricks.

Remember to put your blocks away!

Why do towers topple?

All over earth there is an invisible force called *gravity* that pulls everything down to the ground. The effect of gravity is strongest in the middle of an object, at a spot called its *center of gravity*. When you put a block on top of a tower, gravity will not pull it off if there are enough blocks under its center of gravity to support it. If you push the tower over, you remove that support, and the tower falls.

What's tall, thin, and has pepperoni?

The Leaning Tower of Pizza!

Center of gravity

A tall, thin object, such as a bowling pin, is easy to knock over. We say it is *unstable*. The smaller its base, the more unstable an object is.

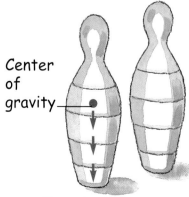

Center of gravity

Base is under center of gravity

Center of gravity

Center of gravity is not supported

A bowling pin falls over if you hit it with a ball because its center of gravity is no longer over its base.

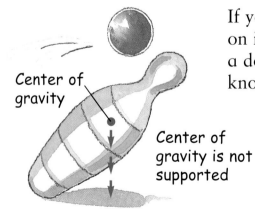

If you stand a domino on its end, it is unstable. In a domino rally, each domino knocks over the one next to it.

See for yourself!

1 Build a tower of blocks, one above the other. The middle of each block is supported by the blocks below. How tall can you make the tower?

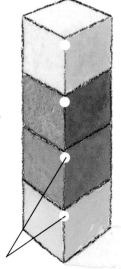

Centers of gravity are above each other

2

Now try to build a leaning tower, with each block sticking out farther than the one below. How tall can you make this tower?

Center of gravity is not supported

3 Blocks can help each other balance, if you put them in the right place.

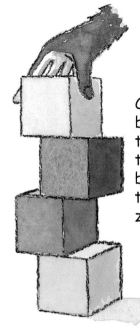

Can you build a taller tower by making the blocks zigzag?

A pyramid is no pushover!

The pyramids built by the ancient Egyptians have lasted longer than many newer towers. This is because a pyramid is a very stable shape. It is wide at the base and narrow at the top. It has a low center of gravity and is always supported by its base. With high centers of gravity and narrow bases, towers are more easily toppled by earthquakes and storms.

Pyramid

Collapsing tower

You can't push wobbly toys over!

Why does clay change shape?

It's fun making things out of modeling clay or play dough. Like the rest of your toys, clay is solid. It will not run onto the floor, like a liquid, or disappear into the air, like a *gas*. If you do not touch it, clay will stay the same shape. But it is soft, so you can change its shape easily by pushing it in and pulling it out. It will stay in its new shape—until you decide to change it again!

Why did the clay change shape?

It wanted to be a model!

See for yourself!

1 To make play dough, mix a cup of flour, half a cup of salt, and a quarter of a cup of water in a bowl. If the mixture is too crumbly, add more water. If it is too sticky, add more flour.

2 Put the mixture onto a wooden board and squeeze it with your hands. Roll it out and use cookie cutters to make different shapes.

Salt

Flour

Water

Rolling pin

Wooden board

Cookie cutter

14

What is clay?

Natural clay comes from the ground. It has been used for thousands of years to make useful things like bowls, jars, and bricks.

Wet clay contains liquid, in which the solid clay *particles* can easily slide into new positions. This is why clay changes shape.

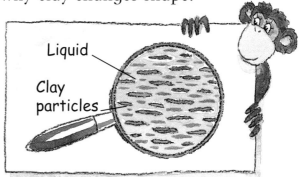

Liquid

Clay particles

You can bend or dent clay, roll it up or flatten it, using either your hands or tools. Shaping clay is called molding.

If the clay dries and the liquid is removed, the solid particles in clay can no longer slide around. The clay cannot change shape anymore.

Clay can be baked hard in a hot oven called a kiln.

Drying rack

WOW!

China tea party

Very fine, white clay is used to make *china*. In the past some dolls were made with china heads, hands, and feet.

China dolls

China tea set

A plastic bag will keep your dough soft.

Can my eyes play tricks?

Have you ever wondered how you see things? Light goes through the front of your eye to make a picture on the *retina* at the back. The retina sends messages to your *brain*, which figures out what you are seeing. Your brain has already learned a lot of different pictures. When you see something new, your brain tries to match what it sees to the images it knows. Sometimes your brain makes mistakes, and your eyes play tricks on you.

What do you see when you close your eyes?

Nothing!

Large or small?

Your brain learns that when things are far away, they look smaller than when they are near you. Our eyes can be tricked to think something is large and far away when really it is small and near.

Could these trees be the same size?

Does Marie really have two tails?

Mirror

Reflections can play tricks on you too. They can make things look different or in the wrong place, or we think there is more of something than there really is.

See for yourself! ✋

1 Sometimes your eyes see something that can have more than one meaning. Your brain does its best to know what you are looking at.

Is this an old lady or a girl with a ribbon around her neck?

2 To make a simple kaleidoscope, find two small mirrors that are the same size. Ask an adult to help you tape them firmly together. Stand the mirrors up.

3 Draw a crocodile head. Put your mirrors on part of the picture and look at the reflections. By putting the mirrors in the right place, you can turn it into a flower.

Simple kaleidoscope

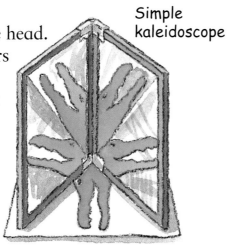

Seeing is believing!

WOW!

Blind people may recognize an elephant by feeling its trunk, but they wouldn't know what it looked like. If they had their sight restored, their brains would have to learn the "picture" as an elephant.

Look! Are your eyes playing tricks?

17

What makes toys go?

Choo-choo-ing gum!

What candy does the toy train eat?

Toys need *energy* to make them go. When you push or pull them along, muscles in your arm turn *stored energy* into *moving energy*, which is passed on to the toys. Toys that move without you touching them get their energy elsewhere. Some toys get energy from the wind, others use *electricity* and need to be plugged into an outlet. But most toys store energy in a *spring* or *battery*. When you switch them on, the stored energy turns into movement, sound, and light.

Energy stores

A clockwork toy has a spring. When you wind it up with a key, your muscles put energy into the spring. The stored energy is turned into moving energy when you let go of the key.

Key

A wound spring stores energy.

I'm all charged up!

Battery pack

Battery

A motor makes the wheels on the robot's feet turn.

A battery-driven toy carries its own stored energy. When it is switched on, the battery turns energy stored in chemicals into electricity. A *motor* turns this electricity into movement.

18

See for yourself! ✋

1 To make a pinwheel, use a piece of thin cardboard four inches square. Make a hole in the center and near each corner. Cut a two-inch slit one inch from each left-hand edge.

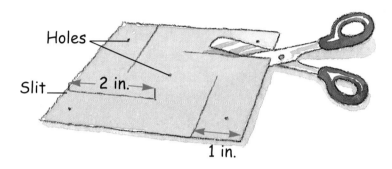

Holes

Slit

2 in.

1 in.

2 Straighten one end of a small paper clip and thread a bead on it. Now bring a corner of the square into the cardboard's center.

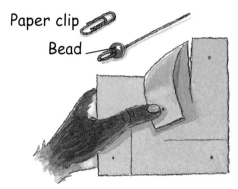

Paper clip

Bead

3 Bring the other three corners into the center. Thread the paper clip through the holes, and hold it in place with another bead.

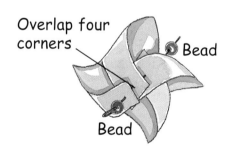

Overlap four corners

Bead

Bead

4 Now twist the paper clip around a small stick, and hold it in place with tape. Make the pinwheel spin by blowing on it or holding it in the wind.

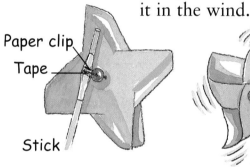

Paper clip

Tape

Stick

Remote control

WOW!

When you use a remote control toy, the handset sends radio signals to the toy to make it move. The handset and the toy are powered by batteries. Different signals may make the toy go faster or slower and turn left or right.

Toys last longer if you take care of them.

How do magnets work?

There are *magnets* in your toys and in many objects around your home. They keep your refrigerator door closed and hold notes on it. They also pick up pins and needles, and they are even at work inside your TV and loudspeakers. Magnets only attract objects made from certain kinds of metal. The most common of these are iron and steel. The pull, or force, between a magnet and the things it attracts is called *magnetic force*.

You're very forceful!

What did the small magnet say to the big magnet?

Magnetic power

When a magnet moves, it comes to rest with one end (pole) pointing toward earth's north. This end is north-seeking (N), and the other end of the magnet is south-seeking (S).

The needle in a compass is actually a tiny magnet. One end always points north. This helps us find our way.

When something containing iron sticks to a magnet, it becomes a magnet too.

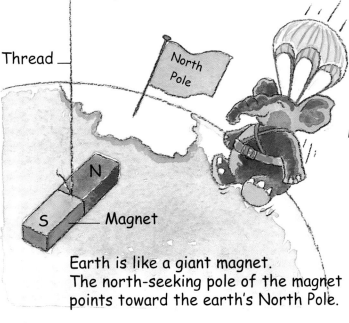

Thread

North Pole

N

S — Magnet

Earth is like a giant magnet.
The north-seeking pole of the magnet points toward the earth's North Pole.

North

West

South

East

A compass

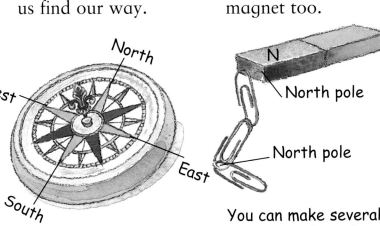

N

North pole

North pole

You can make several paper clips hang from the same magnet.

See for yourself!

1 Put a refrigerator magnet or a paper clip on top of a cereal box, and hold a strong magnet inside the box. Whenever you move the magnet, the refrigerator magnet on top follows it.

Strong magnet

2 Now try using a copper penny. It won't work, because copper is not magnetic, unlike iron or steel.

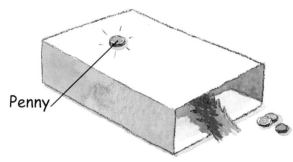

Penny

3 To make a theater, make some scenery to stand behind your box. Draw a figure, such as a ghost, on folded paper, and tape a paper clip to its base. You now have a little puppet to glide over your stage.

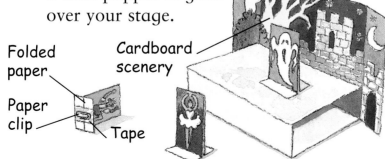

Folded paper

Cardboard scenery

Paper clip

Tape

A rocky compass!

WOW!

North

Some rocks containing iron also act as magnets. One of these, called lodestone, was used as a compass in ancient China. Magnets are named after Magnesia, a place in ancient Greece where lodestone was first found.

Never hold a magnet too close to your TV or VCR!

21

How does my toy crane work?

What did the truck say to the crane?

Can you give me a lift?

Gravity pulls things toward the ground, so they don't float off into space. Gravity also gives things their *weight* and makes them either heavy or light. In order to lift something up, we have to use a force that pulls against gravity. *Machines* make our work easier. A crane is a machine that helps us lift and move very heavy objects that we cannot lift by hand. It has pulleys to help it do this.

Lifting loads

The more rope there is to pull, the easier it is to lift a load.

Pull

A pulley is a wheel with a rope around its edge. By pulling down on the rope, the load lifts. It is easier to pull down than to lift up.

A crane can lift a heavy load and put it down somewhere else. When you wind the rope at one end, it lifts the load at the other.

Pulley

Rope

Hook

Load

Handle to wind rope

See for yourself!

1 Thread a shoelace through a short piece of straw, and put the straw through the middle of an empty spool. Tie it to the rung of a chair.

Chair

Empty spool

2 Thread another empty spool, and tie it firmly around a plastic tub. Put two building blocks in the tub, and put it under the chair.

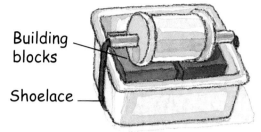

Building blocks

Shoelace

3 Tape one end of a long strip of paper to the top spool. Slip the other end under the lower spool and up and over the top one. Pull gently. The tub will lift easily.

Lift

Chair

Pull

4 Now unstick the paper. Attach one end to the lower spool, pass the other end over the top spool, and pull. Do you have to pull harder than before to lift the tub?

Lift

WOW!

A newton of apple!

In 1665 Sir Isaac Newton discovered gravity when an apple fell on his head. Force or weight can be measured in newtons—and an apple weighs about one newton!

The load must be lighter than the crane!

How do wheels work?

What do you call a broken go-cart?

A stop-cart!

A wheel is round, and it turns on an *axle* going through its center. Wheels help things move over dry land. A sled has runners instead of wheels and will slide over snow or wet mud. But it does not go over rough ground easily. Bumps and stones catch on the bottom and cause *friction*, which slows the sled down. A wheel uses friction to help it turn and move along. The *tire* around the rim has ridges, which help it grip the ground.

Going smoothly

Friction stops things from sliding, but it also helps wheels move. The lowest part of the tire grips the ground, then lifts off as the next part comes around.

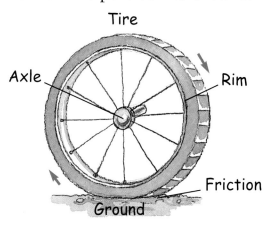

Tire

Axle

Rim

Friction

Ground

Ball bearings are small steel balls. They are usually found in a ring around axles to help wheels turn smoothly.

Ball bearings

You get a bumpy ride if the axle does not go through the middle of the wheel. This is because when the wheel turns, the axle moves up and down.

24

See for yourself! ✋

1 To make a matchbox car, you will need two small matchbox covers. Cut notches at the end of one. Then cut and fold under half the top at the other end. Do the same with the second cover.

Notches

Cut here

Fold under

2 Slide both covers onto one matchbox drawer. Tape a strip of paper around the boxes to hold them in place. Give your car a push. It slides like a sled, but not very far.

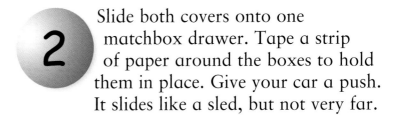

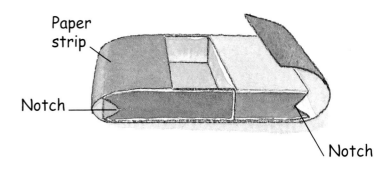

Paper strip

Notch

Notch

3 Cut two pieces of a plastic drinking straw, and put them through the notches at the ends of your car. These will be axles for your wheels.

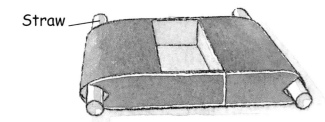

Straw

4 Push four buttons with loops into the ends of the straws. Give your car another push. With its wheels, it will go farther and faster.

Button

WOW! Rock and roll!

Stone block

Sled

Tree trunk rollers

Before the wheel was invented, builders used sleds to move large stone blocks. Tree trunks were used as rollers to reduce friction.

Brakes use friction to stop your bike!

What makes my top spin?

What did the top say to the race car?

Let's go for a spin!

Have you ever made a toy pinwheel spin around by blowing on it or watched a yo-yo spin as its string winds and unwinds? A wheel spins when a motor turns the axle or when you push it along the ground. A spinning top is like a wheel turned on its side. Its axle is vertical, so its rim does not touch anything. You make a top spin by moving the handle quickly, which turns the axle. The faster you make the top spin, the longer it stays up.

How a top stays up

A top falls over when it is not spinning because its weight, acting through its center of gravity, is high up, and its base is too narrow to support it.

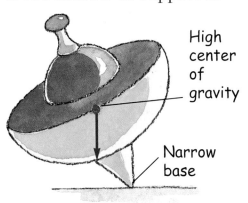

High center of gravity

Narrow base

Center of gravity stays over base

Handle

Axle

While a top is spinning, it moves so that its weight is always over its base, and it cannot fall.

A humming top makes a sound because it has holes that make the air around it *vibrate*.

Air hole

See for yourself!

1 To make a spinner that whistles like a humming top, draw around a saucer on a piece of cardboard and cut out the circle.

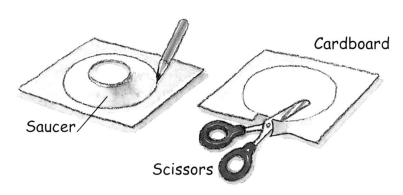

Cardboard

Saucer

Scissors

2 Use a hole punch to cut a ring of holes around the circle. Make two more holes in the center, and thread through a long piece of string.

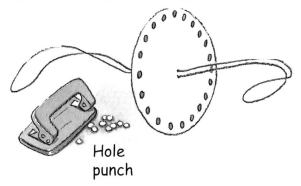

Hole punch

3 Twist the string by swinging the spinner around about 20 times. Pull the string tight, release it, and then pull again. The spinner will whiz around and whistle.

The spinner should be in the middle of the string.

4 Make a spinning top by pushing a pencil stub through the center of a small disk of cardboard. To make it spin, twist the pencil as you drop it onto a smooth surface.

Use colored pencils to decorate your spinner.

WOW! Perfect balance!

A gyroscope is a heavy spinning top that was invented in 1852 by the French scientist Jean Foucault. When spinning, it is very stable. It stays pointing in whatever direction it is put, so it can be used like a compass on ships and planes.

Look for other things that spin!

27

Which toys make noise?

Noisy toys are fun! Rattles, toy trumpets, and drums have something in common. When you play or shake them, they squash and stretch the air around them, making it move back and forth. This makes vibrations, which reach our ears as sound. If a vibration is trapped inside a space, it gets stronger, or *resonates*, and the sound we hear gets louder. Musical instruments are shaped to let this happen.

Which is the noisiest pet?

A trum-pet!

Something in the air

Percussion instruments, such as xylophones and maracas, are shaken or hit to make them vibrate.

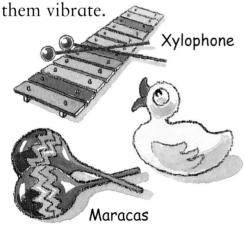

Xylophone

Maracas

Strings

Air vibrates when the strings on a guitar are plucked. The large body of the guitar has space for the air to resonate.

A motor makes this toy car vibrate.

Any toy made of material that will vibrate can make a noise. Moving parts inside toys can cause noisy vibrations.

See for yourself! ✋

1 Although you can't see air vibrating, you can hear it! Collect a selection of bottles, and fill them partly with water.

Fill the bottles to different levels.

2 Now blow across the top of one of the bottles. With a little practice, it will play a note. By holding it when it is resonating, you can feel the whole bottle vibrate.

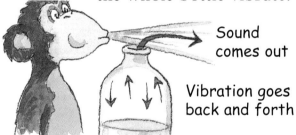

Sound comes out

Vibration goes back and forth

3 To "retune" a bottle, add more water or pour some out. Arrange the bottles in a row to make a bottle organ.

Too soft for sound

WOW!

Soft, rough surfaces absorb sound energy and cut out resonance. Carpets, curtains, wallpaper, and furniture all make your play room a quieter place.

Empty rooms have an echo.

29

Toy quiz

1 What color light does red paint reflect?
a) Red
b) Blue
c) Black

2 What do we call an object that falls over easily?
a) Stable
b) Strong
c) Unstable

3 What happens to clay when it dries?
a) It gets softer
b) It gets harder
c) It turns into a gas

4 In which part of your body is your retina?
a) Your ear
b) Your foot
c) Your eye

5 Where does a clockwork toy get the power to move?
a) From a battery
b) From the sun
c) From a spring

6 What kind of metal do magnets usually attract?
a) Silver
b) Gold
c) Iron

7 What do you use to lift something off the ground?
a) Friction
b) Force
c) Pressure

8 Where is the axle of a wheel?
a) At the center
b) Around the edge
c) Between the center and edge

9 What is a gyroscope?
a) A heavy spinning top
b) A kind of roller skate
c) A musical instrument

10 What happens to a vibration trapped in a space?
a) It gets stronger
b) It gets weaker
c) It stays the same

30

Answers on page 32

Glossary

Absorbed
When light is taken in and not released.

Axle
The rod on which a wheel turns.

Battery
An object containing chemicals that store energy. The energy can be released as electricity.

Brain
The part of the body inside the head that receives information and tells the rest of the body what to do.

Center of gravity
The part of an object where gravity is strongest.

China
Very fine pottery that is made from baked clay.

Electricity
A type of energy carried by a conductor, such as a metal wire.

Energy
The ability to do work or take action.

Force
A push or pull that can change something's movement or shape.

Friction
The force that tries to stop two surfaces from sliding over each other.

Gas
Something that has no fixed size or shape and spreads out to fill the space it is in, like air.

Gravity
Earth's downward pull, which makes things fall.

Machines
Structures or objects used to increase force and make work easier.

Magnetic force
The pull between magnets and the metal they attract.

Magnets
Special pieces of metal that attract objects containing iron or steel.

Mass-produced
Made in large numbers, usually by machines.

Molded
When the shape of a soft material is changed by a force on it.

Motor
A machine that changes electrical or chemical energy into moving energy.

Moving energy
The energy that an object has because it is moving.

Particles
Very small parts of something.

Percussion instruments
Musical instruments that make a noise when they are hit or shaken.

Pigment
A substance used for coloring.

Plastic
Man-made, solid material, made from oil, which can be colored and molded into many shapes when hot.

Primary colors
The colors (of pigments or light) that can be mixed together to make all the other colors.

Reflected
When light or sound is bounced off a surface.

Resonates
Vibrates in such a way that the vibrations get stronger.

Retina
The layer at the back of the eye that sends messages to the brain when light falls on it.

Spring
A coiled piece of metal that stores energy when it is wound up, squashed, or stretched.

Stored energy
Energy that is contained in things (like a battery). Stored energy can be converted into other forms of energy.

Tire
A solid band or air-filled, rubber tube around a wheel's rim, which helps it grip the ground.

Unstable
When something moves out of position easily.

Vertical
Completely upright—straight up and down.

Vibrate
To move back and forth quickly.

Weight
How heavy something is because of the effects of gravity.

Index

Answers to Toy quiz on page 30
1 a **2** c **3** b **4** c **5** c **6** c **7** b **8** a **9** a **10** a